Timeless Presence

Nome

Published by
Society of Abidance in Truth
1834 Ocean Street
Santa Cruz, CA 95060
www.SATRamana.org

Copyright 1996 Society of Abidance in Truth
Second Edition 2003
All rights reserved

Foreword

It is a marvel when Bhagavan Ramana appears in our waking dream. Be it a spark, which is ignited through a spontaneous meditation on Reality, or through hearing the Teaching of Nonduality for the first time and having it strike a deep cord within us, it is unmistakable. It is truly a wonder of wonders when that spark of Knowledge is kindled through constant exposure to the Teaching of Nonduality by consistently listening to it, reflecting upon it, and by deep Self-inquiry upon the Truth of our Being. But it is the most wondrous of all when Bhagavan Ramana makes his timeless presence completely known in Self-Realization.

Presented here is an expression of Bhagavan Ramana's Grace appearing in a life. It is an expression of an inner journey, a glimpse, as it were, into the nondual aspiration of a seeker and the intrinsic essence of a jnani—into the essence of Bhagavan Ramana's Timeless Presence.

This composition was penned at the request of V.S. Ramanan, President of Sri Ramanasramam in 1996. He asked the author to write an autobiographical sketch about "how he came to Sri Bhagavan" so that it could be included in a souvenir book along with other devotee's writings to commemorate the centenary celebration of the arrival of Bhagavan Sri Ramana Maharshi at Arunachala. Out of respect and love of those spiritual beings so dedicated to preserving Bhagavan's Teaching and devotion to Sri Bhagavan, and for no other reason, the author responded to his request.

What is different about this autobiography is that it leaves one with the feeling that the "person" writing it is totally absent, for it is devoid of a "story" about a "life" of a nonexistent, embodied, willful character possessing an outer life in an unreal dream.

What is expressed here will convey to the reader the unequivocal eternal power of the Absolute—Sri Ramana's Presence—as well as extol the infinite love of and complete devotion to such.

It will provide the reader with a deep sense of what is meant when Sri Bhagavan says: "Self is only Being—not being this or that. It is simple Being. Be, and there is the end of ignorance."

Sasvati

Silence. Absolute Silence. Eternal Silence. This is Sri Bhagavan's Presence. Unfettered by time or space, this Presence transcends the illusory boundaries of life and death. Making itself known, it destroys delusion and bondage and brings liberation from all imagination, from all that is unreal. Sri Bhagavan's Presence is the Presence of Siva himself, the Reality of Brahman itself. The effect of His perpetual Silence is impossible to measure as the Silence itself is beyond all mental conception. His every word, glance, and motion is permeated by this Silence, yet the Silence itself is indefinable, ungraspable, in terms of body, speech, and mind. In this Silence, delusion evaporates and illusion vanishes. His silent Presence allows no one to stand apart from it. One is altogether consumed; the only complete knowing of this Silence is in direct experience in which the individual is no more. In this Silence, no notion prevails—not even the slightest trace—and its flood of peace and unalterable happiness completely eliminates the individual and its labyrinthine tale of unendurable lives and deaths without number. In this Silence, all that is objective and the "I" return to their source, and the birthless, deathless, creationless Reality comprehends itself. In this Silence, the only Reality, nothing else has ever been, is, or will ever be.

His Grace is unbounded. It operates in countless ways incomprehensible to the mind. Its scope, touching and illuminating so many lives in so many ways, whether recognized for what it is or invisible to the ideas of the perceiver, causes one to stand in thought-free awe for a timeless moment before prostrating, without hesitation, in full blissful namaskaram. His Grace knows no impediment, because of its omnipotence and its omnipresence. His Grace, which is identical to His Presence, is ineffable in its blissfulness, inconceivable in its vastness, unfathomable in its depth, immeasurable in its compassion, illimitable in its power, indisputable in its Truth, and unalterable in its eternity.

By Grace alone is Liberation from the imagined bondage attained. By Grace alone is there Realization of the true Self. By Grace alone does meditation occur and the profound inquiry, "Who am I?", succeed in awakening one from the dream of an ego with its illusory world-appearance. By Grace alone devotion arises in the heart. By Grace alone are there freedom, happiness, and peace.

With Grace, He has revealed the teaching, which is the direct experience of Reality and the quintessence of Advaita Vedanta. It is the Self's own Knowledge of the Self, of the nature of Being-Consciousness-Bliss. In graceful Silence, He revealed it—His own Existence—and by His Grace, His precious words of instruction have been preserved in the hearts of disciples and devotees. The very books and pictures that are so sacred to all of us are due to His Grace. That we should have the opportunity to see them, to meditate upon them, and to experience their significance is completely by His Grace alone. To our Guru, "the Master without rival," we can never be too thankful.

His Wisdom is supreme. Not a question or doubt, misconception or notion, sankalpa or vikalpa, misidentification or attachment, can remain when His Wisdom is met. There is nothing like it. There are doubtlessly sages who realize the identical, blissful Knowledge, but there is nothing similar to that which when realized is sole-existent. In nonduality, there can be no comparison or contrast, for there is no differentiation. This Self-Knowledge is perfect, and there is nothing beyond it, for it is that in which Knowing and Being are one and the same. If one neither adds to it (appends a limiting notion to it) nor subtracts from it, the perfect fullness shines resplendently. The Maharshi reveals this Self-Knowledge always. In it, there is neither duality nor the triads, neither concept nor anything else. Though the Self is nonobjective, He nevertheless reveals it in utter clarity. Though, in Truth, there are not two such things as path and attainment, He nonetheless reveals the way to abide steadily in that blissful, true Knowledge for all of us and guides His disciples and devotees in a divine, unfailing manner, enabling them to know the unknown Knower of all. With this Knowledge, there is nothing else to know, and the peaceful Bliss that is continuously experienced leaves no other happiness to be desired.

I cannot say when I first met Bhagavan or when the Maharshi's Presence first started to influence the life or when He first "came to me." To say it happened suddenly seems to deny His ever present nature; to say it happened gradually seems to deny the evident fact that He is always present in His entirety. To speak of a sudden event or of gradual growth of that Presence in this life has no rationale. There were memories from before and a distinct, vivid feeling of familiarity with places, images, words, etc., associated with Sri Ramana, as there must be for ever so many disciples and devotees. Yet to place emphasis on such here would seem to accord some dust of belief in an ongoing jiva, which His Grace and Truth have irrefutably proved to be nonexistent. For us with a life in His Grace and Truth, every moment is profound. Each moment, He reveals Himself anew in His entirety, beyond the illusions of time conjured up by the mirage of the mind, and always what is revealed is the ever-same Self. It is neither new nor old, neither reached nor ever lost, but ever the case, with Self, or Brahman, the Knowledge, and our Bhagavan indistinguishably one—utterly indivisible. I can only say that He has always been there. There was a time when that Presence—the perfect fullness of Truth and Grace—was not known. Then it revealed itself. The one who did not know, his ignorance, and his time, being unreal, simply vanished by the illuminative power of that Truth and Grace, of Bhagavan. The joy of the disciple consists in his unimportance and nonexistence, while the sole existence and all-importance of his Guru is his nondual Bliss. Sometimes, one hears a seeker ask if there is a stage at which the Guru is no longer necessary; the answer is that a stage is reached at which the disciple is no longer necessary.

Hearing a story is captivating to the mind. If the story is endowed with wisdom, such as are the stories told by Vasishta and the episodes related in the Upanishads—and, of course, the sublime story of our Guru, the Maharshi—the mind is led by the story beyond all stories. It is just as when a decoy deer has been displayed to capture the deer. Any story about a disciple or devotee serves only to further glorify the wondrous Guru. We do not focus upon the transitory, illusory body of the disciple or devotee, or upon the dreamlike illusions of the events and objects depicted in the story, or upon the unreal personality and individuality of him or her. Rather, we find ourselves reveling in the liberating Presence of the Guru, our Bhagavan, immersed in His sweet Grace, with each story being in some way our own.

Whenever I am asked to give some story that pertains in the least to "my life," there is the distinct feeling that there is nothing to be said. This is so because, firstly, all the events can be told from ever so many perspectives; secondly, because the events themselves are unreal; and thirdly, as disciples and devotees, our only real story is our dissolution in and merger with Him, "like a river when it joins the ocean." Fourthly, there is truly no one born, living, or dying about whom to say anything—the unreal adventures of a phantom man in the city of the clouds. Moreover, once the Maharshi's story is heard or read, who would care to listen to or read any other? Yet, I, myself, am always thrilled to hear any anecdote about anyone touched by His Grace and Knowledge in any manner whatsoever. So, if there is anything said here that can serve the function of reminding a fellow disciple or devotee about the immensity of His Grace and the importance of the Knowledge that He reveals, this will have served some useful purpose; but if any emphasis would be placed upon this body or if there would arise any fascination with a supposed individual, such would run contrary to the intention in saying these things, the intention of him at whose request this has been written [i.e. the President of Sri Ramanasramam], and the Truth itself. What is presented here are more a few descriptions of what has occurred inwardly than any depiction of an outer tale of events, actions, or circumstances. Whatever is declared here is Sri Bhagavan's alone and does not indicate, in the least, any individual's significance, but only the glory of the timeless Presence of the Maharshi. It is said that not a stone on holy Arunachala was untouched by His feet; I am just one of those stones.

It does not seem possible to determine when illusion (maya) began, with all its confusion and bondage. If an inquiry is made as to its nature, it vanishes and proves beginningless in the sense of never having begun at all. With true Knowledge, it is found to be nonexistent. It never came to be, like the illusory snake where, in fact, there is only a rope. There is no actual happiness or peace in illusion. Delusion spawns desire and fear, anticipation and hollow memories, and attachment and aversion as one yearns for happiness, expecting to obtain from someone or something else what is actually one's own. Life appears confusing and binding, while death appears fearful and inescapable. There seems to be no access to the Truth, and the purpose of life remains unknown or forgotten. Even if some word or symbol pertaining to the Truth is presented, there is no ability, it seems, to retain it, let alone comprehend and abide in its true significance. It is a turbulent ocean, mirage-like in nature, with billows of sorrow and troughs of boredom. It is an empty prison without walls and a dream without beginning and end. Meetings are transient, and separation is forever, and though there may be an agreement of deluded ideas, there is no true love. Like dry leaves before gusts of wind, one is driven by karma as one tries to cling to what cannot possibly last and attempts to avoid the inevitable. One learns and learns as life slips by, but no real wisdom is forthcoming, and one never thinks to look within. There is the fear of loneliness that could swallow one up, but one never inquires to see just what it is that is there when, consumed, you are all alone. The description of delusion could go on endlessly, as repetitive as the ignorance itself, but when the Truth is known, Self-revealed by the Grace of the Guru, the whole of illusion is mere nothingness with no duration. Though illusion is nothing, it seems so powerful and encompassing; though it seems powerful and encompassing, it is really nothing.

The Grace of the Guru pierces illusion's bubble-like dream in inexplicable ways. It is always blissful and liberating. It reveals itself as direct experience and shines as revelation. It manifests as sudden samadhi, transcendent of the body and all thought, with no apparent previous cause or condition. It displays itself as myriad lessons of wisdom, the essence of which is always the Knowledge of oneself. It aligns all the factors of life and also lifts one quite beyond them. Though, for many, all these things happen after seeing some passage of His teaching or being blessed by His darshan through a picture or having seen Him when His body still lived, Sri Bhagavan also manifests His Grace in all these ways prior to one's knowing anything about Him, even His name, and only later makes known to the disciple or devotee His name and form, which for us is the name of the Ineffable and the form of the Formless. In His inscrutable, divine guidance, He accomplishes what needs to be accomplished at the perfect time in the perfect way. Thus, in all these ways and more, this Presence manifests. "Unasked, Thou givest." By not erroneously claiming any of these blessings as possessions of the ego, they endure and are not lost to obscuring vasanas. They are identified as being of the Grace of the Maharshi and are not imagined to be the result of fate, of one's own merit, or of the mind's activities or meandering. They shine due to the boundless power of vivid Reality, which Sri Ramana, Himself, is. His Presence manifests, yet may not be known at first to be Him in the sense of knowing anything about a Guru or the Self, let alone having any idea of finding and devoting oneself to that Guru or having the ability to abide as that Self. Later, one learns of that holy name, "Bhagavan Sri Ramana Maharshi," and gains the darshan of that most serene, bliss-bestowing gaze. Then, the heart is flooded with joy, and the path that seemed winding and as narrow as the "razor's edge" becomes straight, direct, and so wide as to make it impossible to go astray.

The Maharshi revealed the secret of Bliss, the real source of deep, lasting happiness. He showed the source, the nature, and experience of happiness to be one and the same. It is not of a worldly or sensory character. Happiness is within. What is within is the Self. "In order to gain that happiness which is the Self one should know one's Self." It seems that this is such simple Truth—and, indeed, it is simpler than any extroverted thought to the contrary—but to fully grasp it and dwell unwaveringly in it is essential. It is foundational to the inquiry into the Self. Hence, He has so clearly enunciated it in the preamble to the sacred set of liberating instructions contained in *Who Am I?*. Once it is truly understood, there is freedom from the world. No longer could anything cause suffering, be it an object, an event, conditions, or a person. With His instruction, the tangled knot of desire and aversion, indeed all attachment, was cut asunder in such a manner as to make it impossible to be recreated. With this simple, profound instruction by Sri Ramana, a direct way to be transcendent of the world was opened that far exceeded the slow approach of dealing with each desire and aversion individually by attempting to remove each thought about such while staying at the same level, or kind of identity, as those thoughts. The detachment thus yielded is of a luminous freedom and peace, the mind's concerns vanishing like the darkness before sun. Wherever and whenever we are, Bliss is with us, in us, and can no more be parted from us than we can be separated from our own existence. The joy of absorption of His teaching and absorption in its profound meaning far surpasses the fulfillment of any desire, even all of them put together. He has revealed Bliss; and with a happy heart, all is at peace.

The entire delusion is said to be the outward-turned mind. The outward-turned mind appears as attachments and misidentifications. The outward tendency has the force of a torrent, but what motivates it, what gives it that force? And how to turn it inward and to turn it inward steadily? Sri Bhagavan revealed the answers in a way that could leave no doubt or difficulty. Indeed, what is unknown to Him, the supreme Rishi, the one who truly knows Brahman for He is Brahman itself? Nothing is unseen by His all-seeing eye. The outwardness is the search for happiness when its abiding place is not known. Further, outwardness is the false belief that the mind's own projections, projected into itself, are real. Finally, outwardness is the wrong notion that there is such a thing as the mind. The Maharshi clearly revealed that since happiness is the Self, the search for it is really the search for the Self, which is the Reality. Happiness, Reality, and the Self are one and the same. When this is known, by consistent meditation on what He reveals even in a moment, outwardness dissolves and the torrent of such tendencies evaporates. It seemed as if the mind went outward, but actually it was only the mind projecting itself into itself, for the whole world is only in the mind and nowhere else. It seemed as if turning inward was like moving a mountain, but He accomplishes the impossible and enables the disciple to find it to be natural.

Turning inward: it is essential. It is the most important thing to be done. By His Grace, it is accomplished. Self-effort is needed. When self-effort meets with Grace, the highest good results. Turning inward, how to go outward is forgotten. Accustomed to detachment, one forgets how to be attached. Immersed in happiness, how to be sad becomes "a lost art," and one cannot be so even in pretense. There is the recollection that once there was suffering, but no actual memory or feeling of suffering itself. Where did the bondage go? I had been tied without a rope. The solidity of the outward turned mind was but imagination. Now, by the Truth and Grace of my Guru, imagination proves causeless and rootless, and the mind returns to its source, like the bird to the boat in a vast ocean, or like a river when it joins the ocean. "Who am I?" becomes known as the only true question, and the yearned for blissful ego-death is here and now.

Bodiless He is, and bodiless He makes us to abide. In some mysterious, inexplicable way, His picture reveals this, with its timeless, Dakshinamurti gaze, just as He explains this with words brimming with compassion again and again to the disciples and the devotees, page after page, day after day. The day the pictures first arrived from Sri Ramanasramam so many years ago was filled with a profound joy. It was the joy of devotion, of faith, of being blessed with the guiding Light, of divine support—in short, the Guru's Presence. There had been no pictures of any kind, spiritual or artistic, anywhere in the place for months. Just blank walls, like a mind that is a clean slate, were there, preparing as it were for His arrival. Then they arrived from His holy ashram on the other side of the world, beckoning me to leave the world altogether. The whole place felt sanctified thereby. The walls and the altar table seemed to support the pictures, but really it was Sri Bhagavan who was supporting them and all else, as well.

If one is going to see anything at all, it should be the divine face of the Maharshi. Silent, it speaks all that need be said to the heart. Like His Teaching, His picture is of perpetual fascination. When I first started to read a book containing His sacred utterances, I had proceeded only about two or three pages before I realized that though, in one sense, I had understood, I had not truly understood. So, I started from the beginning again. This happened several times. Eventually, I realized it was all right to proceed further into the book, but the lesson had been learned. This was not mere inspirational reading, even of a scripture declaring ultimate Truth. This was a means of darshan, and if I could really, experientially comprehend even a phrase of it, the Truth would be revealed and all that is to be known would be known. The perpetual fascination still remains. It will always. Ever new, ever the same, are His Wisdom and His timeless Presence.

"You are not the body." How could a transitory, objective, sporadically appearing, inert form experienced only in the waking state of mind by dependence on the senses, prana, mind, and ego be my real, continuous, nonobjective existence, which is evident without recourse to anything else and is always present regardless of the states of body and mind? And how could that which was already being experienced have remained as if unknown or unrecognized? In delusion, the Real is as if unreal or unknown, and the unreal seems as if real. But Bhagavan, the divine Guru, reveals Himself, and the unreal vanishes as unreal, and thus the Reality remains unobscured.

The body was afflicted by asthma. At night, I did not know if the next breath would come. The medicines did not work, and the side effects of those medicines available at that time could be as lethal as the disease itself. It was all so obvious that life is short and fleeting, and that death comes quickly and unexpectedly. It was doubtful that the bodily life would survive to adulthood, and the physicians yielded to their despair. At the time, it seemed as if I were left with a choice. On the one hand, I could pursue a search for some kind of cure that would hopefully be found somewhere. If a cure were found, life might be extended so that spiritual practice could continue. If the attempt failed, the remaining moments would have been wasted, the life lived in vain, and the only vow I took, the only one Bhagavan demanded—the vow for Liberation (Moksha)—would be left unfulfilled. On the other hand, I could stay put and pursue spiritual practice as He revealed it with all the energy I could muster and adhere to the Truth of the bodiless Self, with full conviction and perseverance, come what may, regardless of the risk. I felt inside myself, "If I do not fully awaken to the Truth, I will live and die in an unreal dream. If I practice right through the last breath, it will all be worth it; and if the Truth is realized even at the last moment, the Liberation from samsara (birth and death) will be for all eternity."

I placed myself in His hands. When the heart's consecration is made, Grace, which is always present, reveals itself wondrously. The intensity yielded the yearned for freedom, and miraculously His Grace made known to me a complete cure for the supposedly incurable disease. He is the immaculately perfect One, the all-knowing One, the ever-same One, the all-illuminating One, and the all-accomplishing One.

Birth, growth, decay, death, pleasure and pains, actions and their results, environments and appearances—all of such are just for the body. The Truth revealed by the Maharshi cuts the knot that seems to tie our true Being with a bodily form. What a relief! What freedom! All the concerns centered around the body had been to no purpose and had been groundless. Illness and pain were no more afflictions. The inert body can move all day, yet stillness prevails, and I never do anything. And the fear of death was gone by His immortality-revealing Truth and His Bliss-bestowing Grace.

The ego, being a vacuous illusion, does not stand alone, but seems to append to itself various concepts, especially in the form of characteristics of a personality. So much of that is associated with the misidentification with the body. With the dissolution of that misidentification, the personality also dissolves. Moreover, the Presence of the Guru brings everything to a cessation. Whether it be before His couch or samadhi, gazing at His lustrous picture, opening a book containing His nectarean instructions, or simply meditating upon His Presence in the heart, we find that the ego and its characteristics and concerns stop dead there and then. The ego falls prostrate, as it were, and cannot continue another step. In that Presence, no attachment can survive, nor can any idea or opinion remain. Nor can any idea of "a world" continue. Nor can past thoughts be recalled, nor future ones come, nor the present ones remain. Nothing can withstand that floodtide of Grace, nor can the ego-mind reach its limit. Like Brahma and Vishnu encountering the infinite linga of the Light of Siva, the mind's creating and sustaining end, and the egoless, infinite Consciousness, self-luminous, reveals itself. The "ability" to be this or that is lost, and the ego lies exposed in its vacuity. How false were all the delusions, fears, and anticipation! They wither and perish by just the slightest touch, in whatever manner, of Sri Bhagavan's Presence.

He liberates one from the corpse of the body, and He liberates one from the phantom of the mind. Having imagined a mind, it seemed as if I were in it, just as it had falsely seemed as if the Self were in a body and in a world when, in Truth, the Self was not in a world or in a body at all. How utterly false proved the mind's fetters and the notion of being in a mind or even being endowed with a mind. Only One who abides beyond the mind can lift one entirely beyond the mind to the Reality of infinite Consciousness. This the Guru mercifully does for the disciple. Only abidance transcendent of the mind can be perpetual meditation and enduring peace. Thought is changeful, moving, and transitory, and lasting peace and undisturbed meditation cannot be found in such. The immovable and immutable, though, is Peace itself. When meditation does not depend upon bodily posture, it endures, and when it does not depend on thought, it becomes perpetual and continuous.

He revealed thought's utter insignificance and that the real Self is all-important. He revealed thought's transience and that Something else within does not rise and subside. He revealed the objective nature of all thoughts (every thought has a form), and the existence of That which is formless and nonobjective. Only the nonobjective is who we are; we cannot be a thought of which we are aware. He revealed the true significance of what Sri Sankara and other sages had referred to as the Witness.

The Witness: it is not a function. It is not an activity. It is not something we do at one time and not at another. It is not an observation process. Because of His abidance as the Self, the Maharshi effortlessly elucidates with the utmost clarity that about which the minds of others might merely conjecture. The Maharshi has revealed the significance of "the Witness," as well as every other description of the Self or the Absolute. Indeed, He is That about which the scriptures speak, and He is the true, inner "translator" within us all who renders the teachings of wisdom and devotion into actual experience. The Witness: it is just Consciousness. It is innately free of thoughts. It is what we are. What the "I" is, is only formless Consciousness. In the delusion of assuming a reality or existence for thought and states of mind, I asked to know this Consciousness in relation to the mind. He revealed it as the Witness, free of the notions of "I" and "this." The only bondage was conceiving the knower to be the known. Thoughts appear and disappear; the Witness remains unchanged. States of mind come and go; that Consciousness remains unaffected. The entire world appears before it and then dissolves; the uncreated and imperishable Consciousness abides as the silent Witness. It is not individualized, being the Witness of all, and is gunatita. Who else but Sri Bhagavan, the ever-gracious and ever-victorious Guru, could lift us out of the grip of the delusive mind with its quicksand-like states and its nonsensical thoughts? Who else but Sri Ramana could show us how to cease imagining corners in the infinite space of pure Consciousness?

Previously, I had hallucinated myself to be in a mind, my mind in a body, and my body in a world. By His clear instruction and world-and-mind-dissolving Grace, I came to experientially know that the world, including the body, is in the sensory experience, the sensory experience is entirely in the mind, and the mind is but "I" in different guises or forms. But, who am I?

The world is only an unreal dream. The "outer" is conceived only in the mind, just as "inner" and "outer" are apparently experienced, but only imagined, in a dream. But, for whom is this dream? It is easy to be detached from an unreal dream that is in no way the source of happiness, but who is detached? Who is bound, and who desires Liberation? Do not cease the desire for Liberation, but simply find out who it is that wants this Liberation or who it is that is supposedly bound; thus you can realize the Truth and be liberated. It is in this manner that Sri Bhagavan has given His Liberating instruction, turning our minds to the source, not allowing them to stray into their own imaginings, and uprooting the very basis of illusion.

Thought ceased. Then it resumed. Again it ceased. And again it resumed. By intense concentration with, and empowered by, the inquiry in meditation, thought could cease. Not just a narrative "voice" dealing with ideas, emotions (which are more ideas), activities, etc., but all thoughts would cease, inclusive of all thought constituting perception and any other kind of thought. But He, the enlightened and all-knowing One, had emphatically declared that what appeared would also disappear. So, if a thought-filled state appeared, it would also disappear. If a thoughtless state appeared it would also disappear. He revealed that that which appears and disappears is unreal. It is unreal not only before it appears and after it disappears, but also for the unreal time during which it seems to be. How can I extend and make permanent this state without thought? That was the idea then. But the Maharshi is always there for the rescue and supplies all the necessary Light and much more. He Himself makes clear (for the understanding of the disciples and devotees, for the teaching itself is always direct and perfectly clear) His own instruction to ease the obtuseness of His disciple—such is His boundless compassion. "Free from thought" had a much more profound meaning, one that is unfading and of the Reality. Awakening to it is abidance free from false definition, modification, and misidentification. Awakening to it, accompanied by ego-death, is the unveiling of the mystery of "no-creation," in which the first thought has not yet occurred. Awakening to it is the entrance into infinite, undifferentiated, space-like Consciousness.

By Grace one is led to peace. Fearlessness itself, Sri Bhagavan, makes one to fear not. Even the fear of death is destroyed. He is the destroyer of destruction, the death of death itself. How much more so is it with lesser fears, all of which are but the notion of the loss of existence and happiness, which are intrinsically one. Because the Self is not known, birth and death appear. If the Self is known, from that moment onward birth and death are gone, and the ever unborn, undying Self remains. Because the Self is not realized as it is, Yama (death) appears, plaguing the inhabitants of all the dreams. Having been plagued for ages, time and again, in a palace of learning with a thousand rooms I traced Yama out by following his muddy tracks. In the innermost compartments, there were three chambers. Entering the outermost one, it was found to be completely empty. Entering the second, it was also found to be entirely empty. In the innermost he appeared, as death is concomitant with the ego. He rushed forward, as Yama cuts down all in no time without sparing any. Only the grace of the Guru can sustain or help one then. His is strength unfailing; and from whom else or from where else can one draw real courage? If one has not embraced the Guru with all his being and if the Guru has not shown the way, how is one to truly face life or death? There is no hope in vain struggle as that is the product of dualism. By His wisdom I knew to hold nothing as myself and to embrace, even death, but, when that is the approach, Yama is powerless and vaporous. Nothing happened. Yama and the fear of death vanished, never to return. I had not done anything. The Lord of all, Guru Ramana, is the one who brings about that which is absolutely necessary and awakens the disciples from this transitory dream of transience. "Those who have great fear of death seek refuge at the feet of the Supreme Lord, the Conqueror of death, who is without birth and death, in order to overcome their fear. They then die to themselves along with their adjuncts (sense of 'I' and 'mine'.) Will those who are (have realized themselves to be) deathless entertain again the thought of death?"

The Maharshi gives instruction about the three states to free us from all that appears in them and to show us that the Self that we are is beyond all the states of mind. Following his instruction, we watch the dream state dissolve, the interim, and the slow creation of what becomes a waking state. Following His instructions, we observe the disappearance of the waking state and the formation of the dream. By applying His instruction, we find ourselves free of both states and all that is conjured up within them. Most importantly, that which is continuous, the one thing that does not change when the states of mind change, becomes evident. Not only does it pass through all the states without itself ever undergoing any change, but actually all the states appear and revolve within it. What is that? It is perpetual Existence. What is that? It is perpetual Consciousness. Like this was the meditation.

Who am I? If only the answer to this is known, there is then nothing more to be known or attained. He said, "The inquirer himself is the answer and there can be no other answer." Who am I? At one point, it seemed the method to quell all other notions, and, indeed, it is ideal for that purpose. Yet, it is still more. It is for the revelation of unobscured Being.

The utter absence of individuality, of the ego, is essential. "The ignorance is identical with the 'I' thought. Seek its source and it will vanish," He proclaimed. "I want to be free of individuality. I may be free of its appendages in the form of various characteristics, etc. but the "I" itself must disappear. How is the elimination of the individual "I" to be brought about?" Like that was the intention and meditation. We should never think that Sri Ramana leaves us to find the answers for ourselves, though that may be said to instruct a person who assumes the Guru will give Self-Realization as if handing over an object. He is always there with the answer, with the ocean of His Grace and the profusion of His Wisdom. We have only to ask the deep questions, and that, too, not merely verbally, but at the same deep level that we wish to experience bliss and peace. His instruction, known to us all, "Can 'I' eliminate itself?" "Find out if the ego does exist" reveals the answer to be closer than I thought.

Myriad lessons about the single sole-existent Reality His Grace and Teaching reveal. He has spoken of Dattatreya, who is associated with the *Avadhuta Gita, Tripura Rahasya*, and pure Advaita. It is said that this great sage of antiquity had twenty-four Gurus. Or it may be said that he had one Guru who appeared in all those ways. Sri Bhagavan, who is Siva Himself, Brahman itself, of an inconceivable nature, is all those Gurus or the One who appears in countless ways. He instructs us by His limitless compassion and love, which humbles us, placing us in awe, dissolving us into nothing so that He alone remains. He instructs us with His expressed Teaching, flawless and all-illuminating. His words are always direct, with nothing concealed or veiled whatsoever. He instructs through the medium of the entire universe, and He instructs by inner revelation and experience. He instructs by the Silence of Reality itself.

The Maharshi's blissful Wisdom is all-comprehensive, making known the nature of everything from the smallest sensation or thought to all kinds of samadhi. No shadow of doubt or confusion can withstand the radiance of the sun of Bhagavan, more dazzling than a thousand suns and consuming the universe in His splendor. Though questions and ideas about samadhi arise for minds not in samadhi, there is no possibility of such notions in samadhi itself. In samadhi, there is no question of effort or its absence, and indeed samadhi can occur with or without preceding effort. Nirvikalpa samadhi had occurred at the commencement of sadhana, just as the Self is already fully present before any of us began our spiritual practice. Some would say that the samadhi was due to hidden samskaras from the past. I would rather say it was due to Grace, for there was nothing else to account for it. Later, with recurring experiences, I would examine to see what brought them about and what brought samadhi to an end. What takes one up, and what brings one down? It helped to eliminate vasanas—misidentifications and attachments. Yet, the Maharshi's revelation of the Truth eliminated the entire field. "Who is the knower?" The questions about samadhi themselves were difficult to raise, for one could not expect to acquire an accurate answer in any less expansive or more formed state of mind, and in samadhi itself the questions would not arise. But Bhagavan is turiyatita and transcends all. He showed that what is experienced—the essence—in samadhi does not come and go; the boundaries constituting the before-the-beginning and the after-the-end appear and disappear, for they are composed only of illusions. "Who goes up or down?" "Who enters into or merges with what?" "Who realizes what?" Oh, the way He cuts every knot and vanquishes every illusion is beyond compare!

    The glories of Sri Bhagavan are endless. Approach Him assuming He has any of the characteristics of a man, and He proves to be transcendent of them all. If you approach as a knower of the Truth, He reveals Himself to be far vaster, as the Truth, Brahman, itself. Then, approach Him as the Supreme Lord, as Siva—as the ineffable, supreme Brahman itself—and He reveals Himself, in all His vast, transcendent nature, to be present moment by moment, even in the most ordinary of circumstances. The anecdotes preserved by those blessed devotees and disciples who witnessed them display this again and again, and we find the same to be true now, His Grace and Wisdom and His Silent Presence with us all the time. "To one who has destroyed himself (his ego) and is awake to his nature as bliss, what remains to be accomplished? He does not see anything (as being) other than himself. Who can comprehend his state?"

Bhagavan is so very thorough. He destroys the root of ignorance, burns up all the branches of illusion like fire when it contacts straw, and reveals the sole Reality in one stroke. He is none other than Dakshinamurti, revealing in one undifferentiated, unbroken, expanse of Silence the natural state of the egoless Self. He provides the support of Grace and the Light of Wisdom. He lays out the direct path—who am I?—and is the ultimate encouragement, while He eliminates the doubt of "Can I realize the Self?" in a way, nondual, that makes it impossible for it to rise again. "Are there two selves, one to realize the other?" His familiar instruction rings in our ears, blowing dualism's dust from our minds, as His silent Presence inundates our hearts. He arranges for everything. We have only to adhere to Him completely, practice His teaching without interruption, and follow His instruction exactly.

Sri Bhagavan has said, "Vichara is the process and the goal also. 'I Am' is the goal and final Reality. To hold to it with effort is vichara. When spontaneous and natural, it is Realization." He declared, "The Self-conscious Being of 'I-less-ness' is the That which is one's true State realized by destroying the ego through Self-inquiry."

Who am I? I could see that the world and the body—all composed of the elements—are not the true Self, do not constitute an ego-self, and are not real. I could see that the senses are not the Self, do not constitute an ego-self, and are not real. I saw that the prana, in all its permutations, is not the Self, does not constitute an ego-self, and is not real. I saw that the mind—all thoughts—is not the Self, does not constitute an ego-self, and is not real. The notion "I" is not the Self, does not refer to any actually existent ego entity, and is itself unreal. "I" does not come from the real Self, does not come from "anything else" (which is imagined only after the "I" is assumed), and is not self-generated. Thus was the experience, without these words or ideas. Who now saw? Who did not see before? "Who is the seer? When I sought within, I watched the disappearance of the seer and what survived him. No thought of 'I saw' arose; How then could the thought 'I did not see' arise?..." He can declare even that which is unutterable, though he is ever Silent.

"The Self is only Being—not being this or that. It is simple Being. Be, and there is the end of ignorance." Truly seeing and meditating even once upon this much of Sri Bhagavan's revelation of Reality—realizing its meaning, supremely profound—the "I" does not survive. It never makes it even to the last sentence. His Wisdom, His Grace, His Presence are all the Reality itself. That is the Self. The Self alone is; there is no other. There is, thus, no ignorance and no separate state of Knowledge, no bound state and no separate state of Liberation. The natural state of nonobjective, uncreated Being has no "other," no alternative. There is no realizer, no "I," and no tale to be told of an "I." There has been no birth, there will be no death. There are no unrealized beings or realized beings; there is only Being. There is no creation. Not a single, objective thing has ever come to be. Being, which is, itself, limitless Consciousness and Bliss, alone is. It is unbroken Silence.

The Guru remains; the disciple disappeared. The Real, which ever is, abides. The unreal, which never is, is said to have gone away. With a heart ever happy and at peace, all events are of no consequence and all opinions are empty echoes. Appearance and disappearance are equal. The wordless, worldless, blissful Knowledge is always, and every day is an utsava, celebration, of Him, the one for whom we have eternal gratitude. There is an indescribable joy in meeting with any of His disciples and devotees, for He is the indweller of them all, and all are one in Him, That itself.

In His great cosmic display of Grace—Nataraja's dance—Sri Bhagavan makes Himself known in ever so many ways according to His own time. It is beyond intellectual analysis. Our illusory bodies, unreal corpses in themselves, are to be regarded just as mere instruments in His hands, so that His truth and Grace should be known—though he does not require us in order that He make Himself known. Whatever is said, He speaks. I have nothing to say myself. To attempt to possess any experience, wisdom, bliss, or freedom is to lose it. Someone may ask a question. The answer is self-evident. There is no one to be a "teacher" or anything else. Moreover, all the trunks of the banyan are one banyan and have no individual existence.

Over the years, this body has been temporarily saved from death and similar things that would have otherwise been considered calamities—disease, accidents, violence, etc. At one time, these would have been conceived as harrowing adventures. The Maharshi's Grace and Truth, though, have not only spared this life, albeit temporarily, but have completely and unfailingly removed any possible fear or suffering. Absorbed in That, there is no second, no fear, and no death. Blissful immortality is a plain and simple fact. Just Being: it is the natural state, the Innate, and that is all.

This is the only time the hand has been put to pen and paper to write like this; and this is only because of the request of one revered by us all, Sri V. S. Ramanan, who is in a blessed line of those who have superbly cared for Sri Ramanasramam, the most sacred place on earth. Indeed, what else can we feel but immense gratitude towards the disciples and devotees who have done so much to preserve Sri Bhagavan's teaching, in the Silence of the Asramam, in the printed word, and in themselves. Incredibly blessed are all the disciples and devotees, and Graciousness itself is He who has bestowed such illumination and peace upon us.

All of the above is, perhaps, more a thin patchwork, a collection of comments, not entirely in chronological order, of an inner life than a recollection of outer events—for the Grace and Truth of the Maharshi are revealed in a manner transcendent of all phenomena. Whatever little is of worth here to one who reads this, it is all of the Maharshi. It can be summed up simply as:

Everything that Sri Bhagavan has said about practice and Self-Realization is true. What He has proclaimed to be real is alone real. It is all true, completely true. There is no doubt of this. Timeless Presence—eternal Truth.

Om Namo Bhagavate Sri Ramanaya

Om Sri Ramanarpanamastu

www.ingramcontent.com/pod-product-compliance
Lightning Source LLC
Chambersburg PA
CBHW062107290426
44110CB00022B/2742